1 PETER

WE ARE REFUGEES

Other studies in the Not Your Average Bible Study series

Ruth

Psalms

Jonah

Malachi

Sermon on the Mount

Ephesians

Colossians

Hebrews

James

2 Peter and Jude

1–3 John

For updates on this series, visit lexhampress.com/nyab

1 PETER

WE ARE REFUGEES

NOT YOUR AVERAGE BIBLE STUDY

JOHN D. BARRY

LEXHAM PRESS

1 Peter: We Are Refugees
Not Your Average Bible Study

Copyright 2014 Lexham Press

Lexham Press, 1313 Commercial St., Bellingham, WA 98225
LexhamPress.com

ISBN 978-1-57-799570-8

Managing Editor: Rebecca Van Noord
Assistant Editors: Lynnea Fraser, Abigail Stocker
Cover Design: Christine Gerhart
Typesetting: projectluz.com

CONTENTS

HOW TO USE THIS RESOURCE

Not Your Average Bible Study is a series of in-depth Bible studies that can be used for individual or group study. Depending on your individual needs or your group pace, you may opt to cover one lesson a week or more.

Each lesson prompts you to dig deep into the Word—as such, we recommend you use your preferred translation with this study. The author used his own translation, but included quotations from the Lexham English Bible. Whatever Bible version you use, please be sure you leave ample time to get into the Bible itself.

To assist you, we recommend using the Faithlife Study Bible, which is edited by John D. Barry. You can download this digital resource for free for your tablet, phone, personal computer, or use it online. Go to FaithlifeBible.com to learn more.

May God bless you in the study of his Word.

INTRODUCTION

I can't breathe. My heart pounds against my rib cage. My mind races, and the ceiling spins. I ask myself all the core existential questions: Where am I? How did I get here? What if I die now? If I only had a year to live, what would I do? While my panic attack only lasted a few minutes, it felt like hours of intense contemplation.

I'm obsessive and pretty high strung. I don't hide it under a calm demeanor—I put it out there: "I'm intense—so what?" But over the years, my drive has been costly. It hasn't cost me a marriage, but I have lost friendships. It hasn't cost me a job—it's probably only helped me vocationally—but it has cost me community. At times, my intensity has also kept me from growing closer to Jesus.

My confession isn't meant to draw pity—and it certainly isn't meant to make you admire my intensity. Rather, it's to show that I can honestly relate to the core of 1 Peter's message: I am journeying through this world of ours, trying to find Jesus, only to realize again and again how far I am from living up to who I am meant to be.

If you're like me, you're slow to offer yourself grace. First Peter is about acknowledging that the only grace worth having is found in Jesus. First Peter is about humbling your mind. It is not about calming down, but learning to rest in God's goodness. In this letter, Peter tells us how to endure struggles, show true love to others, follow leadership, and lead others.

In this study, we will learn that no matter what we encounter, it is possible to find peace in who God is and what he wants to do. There is a way for us refugees on this earth—us Christians—to find "home" in Jesus.

1 PETER 1:1–2:12

Our newsfeeds fill with stories of humanity's depravity. Then our friends share how their spouses and loved ones have wounded them. Once again, our church seems to be going down the wrong path. What can one person do about all of this mess? "I can't even get my own head clear," we think, "so how can I help anyone else?"

First Peter has answers. Writing to persecuted Christians (perhaps around the early AD 60s), Peter says that there is hope. By the great mercy of God our Father—and by the power of Jesus Christ, our Lord—we can pull out of this, even if "this" involves violence against us. Peter explains that we're made to change our world. We *can* take action—action that starts with Christ changing us. We then have to work out the steps toward our transformation as we cling to him—finding Jesus in the pain as he provides the strength to overcome.

What if the war we feel inside is really caused by us—as individuals, as churches, as humanity? And what if it could be overcome by the power of Christ? Peter says it's possible, and then he shows us the way. Let's take a closer look at his hopeful message.

BORN TO LIVE

 Pray that God will give you wisdom as you study 1 Peter.

Read the entire letter of 1 Peter aloud in one sitting.

First Peter was written to a group of churches. The letter would have been circulated to different communities and read aloud. Reading the letter aloud will help you experience it in a similar way to the people who first received it.

Underline each time Peter says "Therefore," "Now," "Dear Friends," or "In the same way." These are key transition words that typically mark the beginning of a new thought. They help us quickly identify the transitions from one section to the next.

What are the primary issues that Peter addresses in this letter? Try to list at least three.

_____

_____

_____

_____

_____

Within the framework that Peter sets up, how would you describe Jesus' message? What is Jesus' work on earth all about—and how does it continue in people who believe in him today?

_____

_____

_____

_____

At what points in Peter's letter did you feel he was speaking directly to you? What do you need to change about your life—or perspective—in response?

_____

_____

_____

ALWAYS BE PREPARED

Pray that God would give you perspective on your suffering and pain.

Read 1 Peter 1:1–2:11. Reflect on 1 Peter 1:1–9.

Peter is an apostle, meaning he is a "sent one"—appointed *by* Jesus to spread the good news *about* Jesus. Peter is writing to "the chosen" living in the listed nations—his key term to describe those who believe in Jesus (1:1). These people live in the "dispersion" (1:1). By dispersion, Peter likely refers to Jewish Christians temporarily living outside of the land of Israel. The term could also be used figuratively to describe Christians awaiting the return of Jesus—living as foreigners in this world, since we belong to God's kingdom.

But Peter offers hope: Not only does God have foreknowledge, but we become more like God through the work of the Holy Spirit—the definition of "sanctification" (1:2). Peter then uses the analogy of the "sprinkling of the blood" to allude to Christ's sacrificial death—casting Jesus' death in terms of Israel's priests sprinkling blood in the front of the curtain of the sanctuary (see Exod 24:3–8; Lev 4:6, 17; compare Isa 52:14). What type of hope do we have—and how do we have it (1:3)?

_____

_____

_____

_____

What has God accomplished "according to his great mercy" (1:3)?

_____

_____

_____

_____

What are the churches in the dispersion dealing with—and how does Peter reframe their situation (1:5-6)?

_____

_____

_____

What will be the result of their difficult situation (1:7)?

_____

_____

How do the churches feel about Jesus and how do they react to him (1:8)?

_____

_____

Does your response to Jesus align with this perception?

_____

_____

When Peter says that the believers will obtain salvation, he is not suggesting that they obtain salvation from their sins through their efforts. Instead, he says that, through their efforts, they will find a way out of their current struggles—they are saved from their circumstances. When they depart from this earth or when Jesus returns again, they know that they will be found in his favor—honored for sticking with Jesus during difficult times. What are some immediate steps you can take to change your perspective on suffering, persecution, and pain?

_____

_____

_____

EVEN ANGELS DESIRE THIS

🙏 *Pray that the Holy Spirit would reveal the relevance of the gospel.*

📄 *Read 1 Peter 1:3–2:4. Reflect on 1 Peter 1:10–12.*

By prophets, Peter is primarily referring to Isaiah, Jeremiah, Ezekiel, and the 12 Minor Prophets (Hosea to Malachi). What did the prophets do for us (1:10–11)?

_____

_____

_____

_____

Read Isaiah 52:13–53:12. How does this passage reflect the message of Jesus in 1 Peter?

_____

_____

_____

_____

Read Luke 24:13–35. How does Jesus reveal himself to his disciples—and what does he show them about who he is?

_____

_____

_____

_____

Reflecting upon this, what do you think Peter means in 1 Peter 1:10–11?

_____

_____

_____

Whom did the prophets serve (1 Pet 1:12)? How do we carry on the prophetic tradition today?

_____

_____

_____

When Peter uses the term "gospel," he is referring to the "good news" that Jesus has come to suffer, die, and be raised again for humanity's sin so that each of us may be saved and have eternal relationship with God (John 3:16–17). How does the gospel endure today—and what phrase does Peter use to note his excitement about the message (1:12)?

_____

_____

_____

Do you anticipate the message of Jesus this way—do you share it like it's this important? If not, how can you change your approach?

_____

_____

_____

GRACE AND REVELATION

Pray that God would help you put your hope in the right place.

Read 1 Peter 1:3–25. Reflect on 1 Peter 1:13–16.

If you had to move quickly in the ancient world, you would tuck your robes into your belt—this was known as "girding up your loins." Peter uses this phrase in 1:13. But here, he refers to our minds. If you want to run fast and hard toward God—and away from evil—you "gird up the loins of your mind." How do we do this (1:13; compare Lesson 2)? How can we more fully rest our hope in Christ, his grace, and his revelation (meaning his return to earth; 1:13)?

_____

_____

_____

_____

_____

What desires do you still conform to that God asks you to change? (List them below.) If you don't already have a trustworthy, Christian friend who you can talk to about these things, find one. By confessing our sins to one another, we can make them transparent—and thus allow the Holy Spirit to overtake that part of our lives. It is difficult to continue sinning when we know someone else is holding us accountable—and when we are no longer living with the shame of our sin.

_____

_____

_____

_____

First Peter 1:16 is a quotation from Leviticus 19:2. How are we to live before
Jesus? What is his desire for our lives?

_____

_____

_____

CITIZENS OF EARTH

 Pray that the Spirit would reveal to you how hope and faith in God should further transform your life.

Read 1 Peter 1:10–25. Reflect on 1 Peter 1:17–21.

If you've lived in a dorm, a foreign country, or a temporary residence, you know what it means to feel out of place. Christian life can often be a lot like that—filled with the sense of "I don't belong here." We are temporary residents here on Earth until Jesus returns or we move on to heaven. How are we to conduct ourselves while we wait (1:17)?

_____

_____

_____

Read Isaiah 53:10–12 and Luke 23. How were we redeemed from our "futile life" (1 Pet 1:18–19)?

_____

_____

_____

Since God has redeemed us, we can know that he believes in us and our potential to change our world. He has hope for humanity and where it can go. Instead of asking, "What do I believe?," we should ask, "God believes in me, how then shall I respond?"

_____

_____

_____

Read John 1:1–4. In what way was Jesus foreknown (1 Pet 1:20)?

_____

_____

_____

Through Christ, we find the ability for all things, including having faith itself
(1:21). Jesus, as one resurrected from the dead, provides the way for us—in him,
we have faith and hope. But not just faith and hope—faith and hope placed
in the very personhood of God. Jesus reconnects finite, sinful beings—us—
with our creator.

In what ways are you living purely as a citizen of this earth?

_____

_____

_____

How can you live more fully as a citizen of heaven who cares about this
earth? How can you enhance your experience in this temporary residence by
remembering the country to which you belong and its king—Jesus himself?

_____

_____

_____

ACTING IN TRUTH

Pray that God would show you how the truth really can bring freedom.

Read 1 Peter 1:13–25. Reflect on 1 Peter 1:22–25.

As a great craftsman, God works on our souls, gradually making us more like him. How are our souls purified, made more in the likeness of God, as he intended us to be (1:22; Gen 1:26–27)?

_____

_____

_____

_____

How should we respond to God's efforts?

_____

_____

_____

The truth allows us to freely live as imitators of Christ. As we become more like Jesus, our concerns about who we are, the purpose of our lives, and any long-term plans are resolved. We can rest firmly in the knowledge that the all-knowing God will reveal himself to us as we pray to him and serve him. In what way have we been "born again" to live this truth (1:23)?

_____

_____

_____

_____

Read Isaiah 40:6–8 and James 1:10–15. How do these passages shed light on Peter's message (1:24–25)?

_____

_____

_____

What has been proclaimed to us?

_____

_____

_____

Are you living as grass that withers or a flower that falls—or in the glory of God? What has more control over your life: the temporary or the eternal?

_____

_____

_____

OF PRIESTS AND BELIEVERS

Pray that God would show you how you can better love other people.

Read 1 Peter 1:1–2:11 once more. Reflect on 1 Peter 2:1–6.

What do we need to get rid of in our lives (2:1)? Based on the context of the book, what does Peter mean by "unadultered spiritual milk" (2:2)?

_____

_____

_____

I remember the first time I had coffee—while camping ("cowboy coffee")—and it tasted odd. It wasn't that I disliked it; I just didn't know what to think of it. When we experience Jesus' work in our lives, it's often a lot like that: At first, it's unexpected and feels abnormal. But over time we experience Jesus' kindness; we learn who he is and what he is all about (2:3; compare Psa 34:8).

Read Matthew 21:33–46. What do you think Peter means when he calls Jesus a living stone (1 Pet 2:4)?

_____

_____

_____

Now, read Matthew 7:24–27 and 1 Cor 3:16. In what way are we living houses for God (1 Pet 2:5)?

_____

_____

_____

Peter says that we are "a holy priesthood"—meaning a priesthood that is "set apart for God." In Israel, the priesthood was charged with upholding the truths of how God desired to be worshiped. These keepers of the temple were stewards of God's work before his people. By applying language formerly used for Israel to the church, Peter shows that God's ministry in ancient Israel continues today. But rather than offering physical sacrifices, we now offer spiritual sacrifices with our actions through truly loving other people— showing them the kind of sacrificial love that Christ has shown us.

Jesus is the stone that all can rely upon and build their lives upon. He is the center of our faith, our high priest (Heb 2:17; 3:1). In what ways can you serve others on God's behalf—more fully living your part in the priesthood of all believers in Jesus?

_____

_____

_____

THE WAR AGAINST YOUR SOUL

 Pray that the Spirit would intercede on your behalf against whatever evil you're fighting.

Read 1 Peter 2:1–12. Reflect on 1 Peter 2:7–12.

Those of us who believe in Jesus have the honor of being a royal priesthood, whose lives are built on the teachings and personhood of Jesus himself (2:7; compare 2:3–6 and Lesson 7). But for those who refuse to believe, Jesus is a stumbling block. (The second part of 1 Peter 1:7 is a quotation from Psa 118:2, and the first part of 1 Pet 1:8 from Isa 8:14–15.) Why is Jesus a difficulty for those who refuse to believe (1 Pet 1:8)?

_____

_____

_____

_____

Peter tells his Jewish Christian audience that they are the extension of Israel's mission—a chosen race, a royal priesthood, and a holy (set apart) nation (1:9). This fulfills what God had told to Abraham and later to King David about their descendants (see Gen 12:1–3; 2 Sam 7:1–16); God always honors his promises.

What does God show us about ourselves and his view of humanity—what has happened to us under Jesus' reign (1:10)? (Compare Hosea 1:9–10; 2:23.)

_____

_____

_____

_____

Many times, we assume that temptations are Satan at work—which in some ways is always true. More often than not, however, we tempt ourselves. We feel pulled in so many directions, and tempted from all angles, because we let evil into our lives. As a result, we let the war against our souls wage on (1:11). This does not mean that we don't expose ourselves to the things of our world; we shouldn't lock ourselves away from the world and its culture. But it does mean that if something is leading us astray—away from God's purposes for our lives—we should change the habit as quickly as possible and be transparent about the problem. We will always find peace in fleeing from evil.

Peter tells his audience—who, though primarily Jewish, are also Christians—to maintain good conduct among non-Jewish people. This gives them the opportunity to articulate the message of Jesus in a convincing way. Serving God is a way to show others who he is and what he is all about—to provide a way for people to come to him (1:12). And if people come to Jesus, they will be present on the day when he returns to earth, and they will glorify him. In what ways can *your* life better glorify God?

_____

_____

_____

How can you end the war waging in your soul? What are some practical steps? (Remember, glorifying God is not just about you—it's also about others and their salvation.)

_____

_____

_____

CONCLUSION

We can feel pulled in too many directions for different reasons. It's often because of self-inflicted temptations and mistakes. At other times, it's because of pressures in our lives or spiritual attacks. But no matter why we struggle, we can have confidence in Christ's ability to calm the situation. In following Christ—as he asks us to—and being transparent and accountable to others, we can find freedom from the things that oppress us. Your mind will be freed up as you humble yourself before God. Center yourself upon the personhood of Jesus—and watch your life transform.

PART II: WE ARE REFUGEES

1 PETER 2:13-4:6

Following a leader is never easy—but it can become unbearable when that leader commits injustices. How can a person live under the rule of a government that does evil? How should Christians respond? These questions don't have easy answers.

Writing to persecuted Christians who are, at the very least, oppressed in words, and likely also in physical actions, Peter tells his audience how to react to society. And Peter knew and understood what he was saying: At the beginning of his ministry, he was persecuted and imprisoned for preaching about Jesus and performing miracles in Jesus' name (Acts 3:1–4:31; 5:17–42).

Our struggles are not just internal, in our minds—they are also external, in the world around us. How are we to live today, in a society gone wrong?

THE INSTITUTION AND US

Pray that even your protests may also honor Jesus.

Read 1 Peter 1:1–4:6. Reflect on 1 Peter 2:13–17.

After reminding us that we are spiritual refugees on this earth Peter tells us how to live. (Peter's audience was Jewish Christians, literally foreigners dispersed from their homes.) Just before 1 Peter 3:13–17, Peter instructs his audience to maintain good conduct before non-Jewish people. This way, when the non-Jewish people slander them as evildoers, the Christians' good deeds may outshine their accusations—ultimately leading the non-Jewish people to Jesus, so that they too may glorify him on the day of his return to earth (1 Pet 2:11–12). Our actions reflect on Christ, so how then should we act? Why should we be subject to human institutions, especially when they commit evil acts against us (2:13–15)?

_____

_____

_____

_____

_____

Peter is not suggesting that evil governments be ignored; if we have an opportunity to change the institution, we should. Instead, Peter is suggesting a peaceful approach that is full of conviction. We might liken it to the approach of Martin Luther King Jr. Until the institution can be changed, practice non-violent protest. Show who you are and what you believe through your good deeds. In this way, Jesus is honored and even those who oppose you will begin to respect you—giving you the opportunity to change your government.

Protest injustice in words, practicing mercy for the oppressed and impoverished and showing respect even to those who commit atrocities against you. In so doing, you may win them over for Jesus too, changing everything. It's a spiritual war of attrition. How should we use our freedom in Christ—and whom do we ultimately serve (2:16–17)?

_____

_____

_____

In what ways does your approach to protest need to change? How can you honor God, care for the oppressed, and bring others to Jesus through your actions?

_____

_____

_____

ENDURING DIFFICULTY FOR CHRIST'S SAKE

Pray that Jesus would show you how to honor him, despite your circumstances.

Read 1 Peter 1:3–3:12. Reflect on 1 Peter 2:18–21.

Why should we be subject to those who treat us unjustly (2:18–19)? Keep in mind that Peter is not dealing with an institution that can be changed—slavery was a major part of Roman culture. He also has a very different kind of slavery (or servanthood) in mind than the one we think of today. This is not the colonial system of slavery; the main kind of slavery in Roman society involved a credit system. In a society with no credit cards or major banks, a person received a loan by agreeing to work for a set period of time for another person. However, some of these "loan officers" (slave owners) appeared to be just and fair but were not.

Ultimately, the biblical view calls for an end to all types of slavery (see Philemon, which points in this direction). For a time, though, Christians needed to endure such institutions for the sake of furthering the gospel. They could not overthrow all things at once—doing so would have resulted in mass persecution and a decrease in the spread of Christinianty. With an eternal perspective, then, Peter writes, "How can we bring people to Jesus here and now?"

How are we to react when others commit violence against us (2:20)?

_____

_____

_____

_____

_____

Read Mark 8:27–38. What does it mean to follow Jesus?

_____

_____

_____

Jesus is calling you—how can you change today to be more like him?

_____

_____

_____

THE SUFFERING CHRIST IS WITH US

 Pray that you may love people as Christ loves them.

Read 1 Peter 2:12–3:12. Reflect on 1 Peter 2:22–25.

Read Isaiah 52:13–53:12 again. It is with these verses in mind that Peter writes 1 Peter 2:18–25. How does the suffering servant—who is ultimately Jesus in the prophesy's fulfilment—react in his suffering? If we were to emulate the suffering servant, what changes would we need to make?

_____

_____

_____

_____

_____

Which verses in Isaiah's prophesy does 1 Peter 2:22–23 echo? How can we live these principles?

_____

_____

_____

_____

First Peter 2:23 indicates that God will ultimately bring justice to those who commit evil. It is not our justice to offer, but his. Even when people hurt us, wrong us, and commit violence against us, we can be confident that God will come through (Rev 6:9).

What verses in Isaiah's prophesy does 1 Peter 2:24 echo? In light of this message, what should be our response—what needs to change?

_____

_____

_____

First Peter 2:25 mirrors ideas from John 10:1–21. Read John 10:1–21. How can we follow after Jesus, the ultimate leader of our faith?

_____

_____

_____

Do you feel that your soul is being overseen by Jesus? What parts of yourself do you still need to surrender to his rule?

_____

_____

_____

MARRIAGES ARE TRICKY BUSINESS

Pray that you may honor Jesus in every relationship, even when it's hard.

Read 1 Peter 3:8–4:11. Reflect on 1 Peter 3:1–7.

Within the same framework—bringing people to Jesus, even with the cost of difficulties—Peter writes 1 Peter 3:1–7: If you are married to someone who does not know Jesus, do what it takes to bring them to Christ. (Peter specifically addresses women in this passage because it appears that a large portion of the New Testament church was women.)

What if you could win someone over to Jesus without speaking a single word? What if a person simply witnessed Christ at work in you and desired to know the God who has transformed you (3:1)? With this idea in mind, Peter suggests that wives—living in a first-century AD, patriarchal society—should not exert their ultimate freedom in Christ over their non-Christian husbands, but instead live in a manner that helps their husbands accept Jesus. After accepting Christ, the wives in Peter's churches will have the opportunity to show the equality that Jesus so desires and offers (3:2). (The exact word used for "submit" here is also used in Ephesians 5:21, 24 to describe the need for spouses to "submit" to one another.)

Writing to a culture that saw a woman's hair as sexual in nature, Peter tells women to let their beauty be shown through their emotional and spiritual intelligence rather than their hair (1 Pet 3:3–4). What would be an equivalent statement today (3:3–4)? If Peter offers the alternative of living with a gentle, quiet spirit, what current alternative would we offer—or is Peter's alternative still applicable?

_____

_____

_____

Peter describes Sarah as an example to his audience: He notes that Sarah called Abraham "lord," a form of polite address like "sir"—an appropriate and applicable term in his culture (1 Pet 3:5-6). Even in some cultures today, it would be appropriate for a wife to address a husband this way. (Similarly, when I travel to eastern countries or interact with eastern cultures, I'm "Brother John," "Sir John," "Pastor John," or "Director John" and likewise address my hosts by their titles. Even though I feel uncomfortable with these terms, it's necessary for maintaining good relationships, and thus furthers the gospel.)

But Peter is not simply concerned with culture. He goes beyond his cultural norms to tell husbands that they should not rule over their wives, but rather should be understanding, showing their wives honor (3:7). When Peter calls women the "weaker vessel" he is not saying they are actually weaker; he is likely referring to their physical build, which would have been noticeably different in a labor-intensive culture. The context of the passage does not suggest that Peter views women as inferior in any way; in fact, Peter indicates that women—despite cultural norms of his time—are heirs along with men (only men in this culture could receive an inheritance). What will happen if a man does not treat his wife with respect (3:7)?

_____

_____

_____

How does your relationship with your spouse—or close friends—reflect the ideals of Jesus' message? In what ways does it need to change? (When answering this question, think about yourself—don't make this about the other person. If you aren't married, think about this in terms of your friendships with others.)

_____

_____

_____

HUMBLE YOUR MIND

 Pray that the Holy Spirit would humble you before his presence—allowing for him to renew your very mind.

Read 1 Peter 3:13–4:11. Reflect on 1 Peter 3:8–12.

What are the four things Peter asks of us (3:8)? What does it look like to practice each of these attributes—and how can you more actively do them?

_____

_____

_____

How should we react to the oppression and persecution of other people (3:9)? What would change about some of your relationships if you reacted the way that Peter recommends?

_____

_____

_____

First Peter 3:10–12 cites Psalm 34:12–16. Read Psalm 34:11–18. How can we practice the principles of this citation? How does God react to people who treat others with love, and seek and pursue peace?

_____

_____

_____

Think about your relationships with those who treat you poorly. How do you currently react to them? What needs to change? How can you live the practices preached in 1 Peter 3:8 in all circumstances?

_____

_____

_____

BEING A CHRISTIAN— IN ALL THINGS

 Pray that Jesus would show you how to demonstrate love to those who treat you poorly.

Read 1 Peter 3:13–22. Reflect on 1 Peter 3:13–16.

If you do well for others, it's difficult for other people to oppose you (3:13). On the other hand, if you do good in Jesus' name and people still treat you poorly, your actions are worth suffering for—and God will ultimately bless you (3:14).

How should we feel about those who treat us poorly (3:14–15)?

_____

_____

_____

_____

Our duty (and obligation) as Christians is to be prepared, in all circumstances, to (gently and with respect) tell others about our hope in Jesus and the redemption he has offered us (3:15). How can you better prepare yourself for this task? What practical steps can you take to be prepared to speak the truth about Jesus?

_____

_____

_____

_____

_____

How can we have a "good conscience" while telling about the message of Jesus (3:16)? (See 3:8–15 and Lesson 5).

_____

_____

_____

How can our positive actions toward Christ put people who persecute us to shame (3:16)?

_____

_____

_____

POWER STRUGGLES AND JESUS

 Pray that God would give you the wisdom to understand the cosmic effects of Jesus' actions.

Read 1 Peter 3:13–4:11. Reflect on 1 Peter 3:17–22.

Drawing on the framework of 3:8–16, Peter offers what may be viewed as a summary statement of 3:8–16 or an opening statement for 3:18–22. What type of suffering should we take pride in—and what kind of suffering should we avoid (3:17)?

_____

_____

_____

Read Douglas Mangum's article, "Preaching to the Spirits," in the appendix. Mangum summarizes the cultural backdrop of 1 Peter 3:18–22:

> First, Peter expands on the implications of Jesus' death and resurrection: at some point, Jesus affirmed the condemnation of the fallen angels who had rebelled prior to [Noah's flood] and had been imprisoned by God (3:18–20a). Peter then employs the analogy of the salvation of Noah and his family through water to describe the salvation of believers through baptism: just as Noah was saved by righteousness, believers are saved by faith; baptism is symbolic of their act of faith (3:20b–21a). Peter emphasizes this by stating how baptism saves by an appeal to Christ's resurrection, not the physical washing of water baptism (21a). Essentially, Christ's resurrection has eternal implications for the divine beings that rebelled against God. The resurrected Christ is now elevated to the right hand of God with authority over all other angelic beings (22).

God is just in his judgment—he even sent his own Son to ensure that salvation is offered to all, even to the spiritual beings who rebelled against God in the beginning and committed incredible atrocities against humanity (Gen 6:1–8). God wishes to see all come to him (2 Pet 3:9). Why does Peter communicate this message to us? What is he trying to explain?

_____

_____

_____

If 1 Peter 3:17 is an opening statement for 3:18–22, what do we know about Peter's reasoning for including this excursus in thought?

_____

_____

_____

How did Christ suffer—and what were the results of his suffering? If we suffer for Jesus, how should we feel about it? What does Jesus' suffering teach you about living for him today?

_____

_____

_____

JESUS GOES WHERE NO ONE ELSE WILL

 Pray that you would understand the cosmic nature of God's graciousness.

Read 1 Peter 3:13–4:6. Reflect on 1 Peter 4:1–6.

How should we think about our lives—and any pain that we may experience (4:1; compare 3:8–22; see Part II, Lessons 5–7)? What type of changes does suffering for Christ effect (4:2)?

_____

_____

_____

_____

_____

Read Romans 6:1–13. How does this passage parallel 1 Peter 4:1–2? What is God's grand vision for our lives?

_____

_____

_____

_____

_____

Peter uses non-Jewish people, Gentiles, as a metaphor for those who do not believe in Jesus. A Jewish-Christian audience would have understood his reference as "people who do not share our beliefs and live as they will, according to the views of Rome and Rome's pagan gods." Roman religion involved all kinds of evil, hence the list of wrongdoings Peter includes in 4:3. This sort of debauchery was culturally expected—not viewed as abnormal, as it is in most modern societies (4:4). What will God ultimately do about the evils committed by people who do not share our belief in Jesus (4:5; compare 3:18–22 and Lesson 7)?

_____

_____

_____

God is gracious—bringing the good news of salvation in Jesus to all people— in order that all people may live as God has asked, in relationship with him (1 Pet 4:6; Gen 1:26–27). How does this cosmic view of God and his work change your perspective on your current circumstances? What vision does it cast into your life?

_____

_____

_____

CONCLUSION

Throughout his letter, Peter weaves a beautiful tapestry of theology, poetry, and practical advice. He offers hope to those who feel hopeless. With tragedy on the horizon, he shows us a new day, lived for Jesus. But this day is ancient: It is cast in the light of all that God has done in the past—from his first promises to Abraham, to the exodus, to the exile, to salvation in Christ, to the day of his return, we see one faithful God leading us forward.

Theologians often look to Romans as the center of the New Testament's message—as the place that brings everything together. But I think we should look to 1 Peter. No other New Testament book brings together theological elements from the Gospel of John, Hebrews, the book of Acts, the Gospels, and Paul's letters—while drawing on the Psalms and Isaiah. Peter tells us: We are born again (as John says), we are living under one priest, "the living stone" (as the author of Hebrews shows), we are the people who implement Jesus' message in the world even under suffering (as Acts shows), and we are fully redeemed in Christ (as Paul shows). All of this is set against the backdrop of the Psalms and God's cosmic action beginning in Genesis, with the creation and the flood. Placed against Isaiah's story of the suffering servant— and as Isaiah himself showed in his prophecy—we see how Jesus is priest, the sacrifice for our sins, and our intercessor: His actions change the very fabric of the world. He makes way for us to have relationship with God once again. He bridges the gap that no one else could—as both God and human.

Within the context of this rich theology, we learn how to live as refugees on this earth—bound for heaven, but with a great purpose while we are here. We can bring others to our Lord, showing them the way through our words and deeds. Eternity is coming, and we have the ability to prepare others. But this also means we must change along the way, to live more like the suffering servant, Jesus, whom we follow.

God wants his grace to be revealed to everyone—will we show it to them?

1 PETER 4:7–5:14

If you knew that the end of all things was at hand, what would you do? This question drives the ending of Peter's letter, when he places us at the judgment seat of God.

Peter has told us what God has done: how he was willing to die for us as a man and was even willing to go to the deepest darkness to proclaim the good news of salvation—and how Jesus is now our risen Lord. Peter has explained what it means to follow Jesus despite persecution and difficulty, and he has shown us the cosmic scope of God's work since ancient times. With this holistic perspective in mind, we are asked how we will respond—and given some very personal advice from Peter on how to live as a believer in Jesus.

Essentially, Peter asks us, "Do you love Jesus, really?"—just like Jesus had asked him (John 21:15-19).

THE END IS NIGH

Pray that Jesus' forthcoming return would be real to you.

Read all of 1 Peter. Reflect on 1 Peter 4:7–11.

By the "the end of all has drawn near" Peter means the day when Jesus will return, when the earth will be made new—with all evil being vanquished, and wholeness and goodness being restored (Rev 21). If a day is like a thousand years to God, then the time when Jesus will return has always been near—since the moment he left (2 Pet 3:8–10). What should we do in light of the reality of Jesus' return and why (1 Pet 4:7)? What should we do above all things (4:8)?

_____

_____

_____

_____

As believers in Jesus, we are to show hospitality to other people, including other believers, without complaint; this is a measure of our faith (1 Pet 4:9; see 2 John).

We are merely stewards of God's gifts (4:10). We each have gifts from God and we're meant to use them to serve one another. If we are gifted with speaking abilities—apostolic ministry, prophesy, evangelizing, or teaching—then we are to use those for speaking God's truth, his very words (4:11). (Peter likely has the specific gift of prophesy in mind). Likewise, whenever we serve others—which is also a spiritual gift—we should do so by God's very strength (4:11; see Phil 4:10–14). What is the purpose of God's gifts to us, and who deserves honor for them (4:11)? Can this also be extended to the purpose of our lives?

_____

_____

_____

Peter's message in this section ends with an "Amen," which simply means "so it is" or "so be it." This likely indicates that Peter has finished a praise song or prayer to God. Do you ever break out in praise for God like this? Do certain moments prompt you to stop and pray?

_____

_____

_____

How can you bring more of these moments into your life?

_____

_____

_____

SAFE, BUT IMPRISONED

🖐 *Pray that Jesus would show you who he truly is and what he desires from you.*

📄 *Read 1 Peter 2:12–5:14. Reflect on 1 Peter 4:12–15.*

Every great story is formed by difficulties—without pain and anguish, our lives lack both adventure and growth. If we're honest with ourselves, our stories can become quite boring: We take the same route to work every day in our "safe" cars with the radio turned up, then sit quietly at our desks. We're afraid of pain, difficulty, and awkwardness. But risk is inevitable—your drive home is itself a risk. And Jesus calls us to risk it *all* for the sake of God's kingdom, for others. Read Matthew 10:16–42. What is Jesus' core teaching about risk?

_____

_____

_____

Trials—as difficult as they may be—can yield results (1 Pet 4:12; compare 1:6–7). Read Matthew 5:11–12. What does Jesus have to say about serving him and what we should expect?

_____

_____

_____

Why should we rejoice in our sufferings for Jesus (4:13–14)? Let this knowledge calm your spirit and mind.

_____

_____

_____

What type of suffering should we avoid (4:15)?

_____

_____

_____

There is pure joy in knowing Jesus, our Lord—and serving him as he intends. How can you move beyond the "safe" to _truly_ following after Jesus? Stop and pray—what is God calling you to right now?

_____

_____

_____

NO SHAME IN THIS

Pray that you would be bold for Jesus, not ashamed.

Read 1 Peter 4:1–5:14. Reflect on 1 Peter 4:16–19.

First Peter 4:16 offers us a difficult message: Contrary to our culture's belief, it is okay to endure persecution without speaking a word of protest. The prophesy about Jesus in Isaiah, echoed earlier in Peter's letter, articulates this: "The servant was oppressed and afflicted, yet he did not open his mouth; like a sheep to slaughter, and like an ewe before its shearers is silent, so the servant did not open his mouth" (Isa 53:7). What should be our ultimate response to suffering for Jesus (4:16; see Part III, Lesson 2)?

First Peter 4:17 may begin in addressing Roman judgment of believers in Jesus, but Peter's viewpoint seems to include the larger perspective that those who do not obey God will ultimately be judged by God himself. Peter casts his overall viewpoint on the matter of the persecution of Christians—and God's ultimate judgment of all—in light of Proverbs 11:30–31; read this passage (see also 1 Pet 4:18). Why do you think Peter sets up his viewpoint this way? What does it mean?

How should we respond to persecution (4:19)?

_____

_____

_____

Read Mark 8:27–9:1. How can you find more boldness in your faith, even when it's difficult? How can you better embrace what it means to follow Jesus?

_____

_____

_____

LEADING LIKE JESUS

Pray that Jesus would teach you how he leads—and thus how you should lead.

Read 1 Peter 4:7–5:14. Reflect on 1 Peter 5:1–5.

The elders whom Peter addresses are church leaders (5:1). "Elder" here doesn't refer to age, but to a position within the community (compare 1 Tim 4:12). How does Peter view himself?

_____

_____

_____

_____

What are the attributes of a godly church leader—and what should church leaders not do (1 Pet 5:2–4)?

_____

_____

_____

_____

Read Psalm 23. Consider the metaphor of a shepherd. In light of this metaphor, how can church leaders be ambassadors for God here on earth?

_____

_____

_____

_____

Jesus is the chief shepherd and our model for church leadership: Each leader serves under him (5:4). In what ways is your leadership in alignment with this principle—and in what ways does it need to change?

_____

_____

_____

When Peter tells younger people to be subject to the elders of the community, he is not suggesting that young people cannot be elders (1 Pet 5:5; Timothy's example proves otherwise—see 1 and 2 Timothy). Nor is he suggesting that leaders can do whatever they wish and others simply must follow (see 1 Pet 5:3). Peter is probably—in alignment with the rest of the letter—telling younger people to respect their community's leadership, as they were using their freedom in Christ as a license to disrespect their leaders. In so doing, their probable actions presented obstacles to others' coming to Jesus (1 Pet 2:11–12). (It was common practice for Jewish leadership to be shown great respect in the first century AD.) How should we show church leaders respect today? What are you doing that could be an obstacle for people believing in Jesus?

_____

_____

_____

OH, HUMILITY—IF ONLY I HAD YOU

 Pray that God would show you where your spirit is out of alignment with him and his purposes.

 Read all of 1 Peter once more. Reflect on 1 Peter 5:5.

The second part of 1 Peter 5:5 reminds us to practice humility—something many of us, including me, struggle with. Read Matthew 20:20–28. How does humility factor into serving God's kingdom?

_____

_____

_____

_____

Read Proverbs 3:28–35. How does God define humility, and how does he feel about arrogance? Ultimately, where does an arrogant attitude lead us?

_____

_____

_____

_____

Read James 4:11–5:6. What does James say about arrogance?

_____

_____

_____

What does arrogance lead us to do? (If we consider ourselves blessed by God because of our wealth, what implications does that view have for the impoverished of our world? How does our perspective need to change?)

_____

_____

_____

In what ways do you show arrogance? How can you alter those actions to reflect humility instead?

_____

_____

_____

WHY OWN WHAT IS GOD'S?

 Pray that the Holy Spirit would give you the ability to cast your burdens upon him.

 Read 1 Peter 4:12–5:14. Reflect on 1 Peter 5:6–9.

What should we do—right here and right now (5:6)?

_____

_____

_____

When we choose to "let" Jesus own our anxieties and cares, we are being arrogant, for he has already owned them on the cross (1 Pet 5:7; Isa 53:12).

Why does Peter tell us to be sober and alert (1 Pet 5:8)?

_____

_____

_____

_____

Do you join your brothers and sisters in Christ in their sufferings (5:9)? Do you view their sufferings as yours—their stories as your story? How can you join them in their efforts to show Jesus' love to the world?

_____

_____

_____

_____

THIS GOD IS MAKING ALL THINGS NEW

Pray that God's infinite perspective would change your life today.

Read 1 Peter 5:1-11. Reflect on 1 Peter 5:10-11.

What will God do for us after our time on earth (1 Pet 5:10; see Part III, Lesson 3)?

_____

_____

_____

Reflect upon the four things that Peter says God will do (1 Pet 5:10). Let these ideas reach your heart and change your outlook. Let them be guiding principles for your life—this is the work God does and will do in you.

Peter offers us a great promise (5:11). Read Revelation 21. What does God's abode look like? What emotions does God's work evoke in you?

_____

_____

_____

If you were standing at the end of all things—when God has made all new—what would you change about your current circumstances? What would you do differently?

_____

_____

_____

How can you practice these actions today?

_____

_____

_____

If we think of the world as God does—as much as we're able to do so in our finite perspective—our viewpoints can be radically altered to be more like his. We can see his power and work in our lives, transforming us. We can live like we believe.

ALL GOOD THINGS MUST COME TO AN END

 Pray that the message of 1 Peter would stick with you—that it may renew your very mind, heart, and soul.

Read 1 Peter 5:1–14. Reflect on 1 Peter 5:12–14.

At the end of Peter's letter, he tells us that that Silvanus transcribed the letter (5:12). What does Peter think of Silvanus? Would others say the same about you?

_____

_____

_____

_____

What "basic" skills could you be using to glorify God?

_____

_____

_____

What is the purpose of Peter's letter (5:12)? What type of actions does he expect us to take after reading it?

_____

_____

_____

_____

In 1 Peter 5:13, "Babylon" is likely a reference to Rome—and the empire's evil schemes and ways (see Rev 14:8). The "she" in Peter's sentence likely refers to the church in Rome. He is probably writing from Rome and uses this cryptic sentence so as to avoid revealing the church's growing presence in the city to anyone who may unintentionally receive his letter.

Peter calls "Mark"—referring to John Mark, one of Paul's early associates (see Acts 12:12, 25)—his "son" in a spiritual sense (1 Pet 5:13). Peter is likely either Mark's mentor or the one who first brought Mark into the Christian faith. Ultimately, Peter tells the believers in his churches to greet one another with a customary greeting to show kindness and respect—"the kiss of love" (1 Pet 5:14).

How does Peter end his message (5:14)?

_____

_____

_____

Ultimately, how are we to respond to Jesus? What are we to feel?

_____

_____

_____

Do you feel this today—if not, what is God calling you to do differently?

_____

_____

_____

We are all a type of refugee on this earth—following after Jesus, as vagabonds. We wander the earth as people meant for something more—heaven—where our spirits will be completely restored to peace, wholeness before God. And it is with the beggar, the refugee, the impoverished, and the hurting that we sympathize and love—for we are all the same in Jesus, our Lord. We sympathize even with those who hurt us, for we too have hurt others and God, yet grace has been given to us in the form of Jesus, the suffering servant.

CONCLUSION

Their clothing is ragged and torn. One man has his hand on the other man's shoulder. Then I see that the shorter man is feeling around in front of him with his hand—he is blind. As they stand at the crosswalk, I realize that the blind man would be walking into the intersection if it wasn't for his friend. With one gentle hand placed on his back, the blind man can see through the other man's eyes. He is safe, even in this dangerous world.

I am like the blind man, and the man with his hand on my shoulder is Jesus—the rabbi, carpenter, and messiah. Jesus is walking with me—through the danger of the intersection and into town. Our clothing is ragged: I am a beggar in this town, asking the messiah for salvation. Jesus is wearing rags because he is homeless, as he was on earth. We are both refugees in this place, even though he is a king. And after my time on earth with him, he is taking me somewhere better. His dad has a place I've heard about—it's beautiful and wonderful. But here in the shadows of this town, I know I have a mission and the only way to get there is to let Jesus' hand rest on my shoulder—to walk me through the pain, anguish, and suffering. I will risk everything for this man, Jesus the rabbi, for he has already saved me.

Without Christ, we can see nothing. With him, we can overcome all things. We can humble our minds, find rest for our weary hearts, and live as we are meant to live. We can be what we are meant to be, one step of faith at a time.

PREACHING TO THE SPIRITS

Douglas Mangum

First Peter 3:18–22 is one of the most difficult passages in the NT to understand due to the cryptic statements of 1 Pet 3:19–20, where Peter describes Christ as preaching to disobedient "spirits in prison"—an event that is apparently linked to the time of Noah and the flood (Gen 6). Various interpretations have been proposed regarding this passage.

One option holds that Christ descended into the Underworld (Sheol, Hades, hell) in connection with his death on the cross. Before his resurrection, while still "in the spirit" (1 Pet 3:18), he made a proclamation to the deceased human souls imprisoned in the Underworld. In this view, the "spirits" in 1 Pet 3:19 are the same as the "dead" in 1 Pet 4:6. Still, some options regarding the identification of these imprisoned souls and the purpose of Jesus' message remain: Christ's descent may have provided the dead of Noah's generation with an opportunity for salvation; alternatively, it may have provided salvation for the OT righteous; or, it brought about condemnation for the unbelieving generation of Noah.

A related view is that the pre-incarnate Christ visited the generation of Noah in their lifetime, rather than in the Underworld after his death, preaching repentance from sin. This view was popular in the medieval era but has largely been rejected by modern interpreters. Essentially, the possibility that souls in the Underworld could repent after death poses a theological difficulty. Given this, another interpretation suggests that Christ descended into the Underworld to announce salvation to the people who had repented of their sins just prior to death.

Most of these interpretations understand the "spirits" as a reference to the souls of the human dead; however, the NT never uses the word for "spirit" in an unqualified fashion to refer to the human soul. Therefore, the reference in 1 Pet 3:19 may point to nonhuman supernatural beings. This interpretation is strengthened when the passage is read in the context of Gen 6–9 because of the reference to Noah and the flood in 1 Pet 3:20. The flood reference also draws in the traditions of 1 Enoch, so the "spirits in prison" may have been understood to be the fallen angels or "sons of God" of Gen 6:1–4. Enoch, as in Gen 5:21–24, prefigures Christ in that God sent Enoch to the fallen spirits—the sons of

God who cohabitated with human women (Gen 6:1–4)—to announce their impending doom (see 1 Enoch 1:9; 10:1–10; Jude 14 and note). For Peter, Jesus is the new Enoch; he proclaimed victory over the powers of evil through his actions on the cross.

These three interpretive possibilities developed out of the various theological questions raised by the passage. Why would Christ preach to imprisoned spirits of the dead? Can the dead respond in faith? By the same token, why would Christ preach to imprisoned fallen angels, emphasizing his victory and their defeat? Despite these questions, understanding the context provided by Second Temple Jewish literature and its expansions on the Genesis traditions offers the closest parallel for understanding the cultural and literary allusions that might have been evident to the letter's original audience: Christian Jews of the first century AD.

As the final option considered above, this culturally anchored interpretation can be summarized as follows. First, Peter expands on the implications of Jesus' death and resurrection: at some point, Jesus affirmed the condemnation of the fallen angels who had rebelled prior to the flood and had been imprisoned by God. Peter then employs the analogy of the salvation of Noah and his family through water to describe the salvation of believers through baptism: just as Noah was saved by righteousness, believers are saved by faith; baptism is symbolic of their act of faith. Peter emphasizes this by stating how baptism saves by an appeal to Christ's resurrection, not the physical washing of water baptism. Essentially, Christ's resurrection has eternal implications for the divine beings that rebelled against God. The resurrected Christ is now elevated to the right hand of God with authority over all other angelic beings.[1]

---

[1]Douglas Mangum, "Interpreting First Peter 3:18–22," in *Faithlife Study Bible* (ed. John D. Barry, Michael R. Grigoni, Michael S. Heiser, Miles Custis, Douglas Mangum, and Matthew M. Whitehead, Bellingham, WA: Lexham Press, 2012).

Make Your Bible Study Even Better

Get 30% off Bible Study Magazine.

Subscribe today!